People came from miles around the village of Much Twittering to buy Betsy Bun's bread and cakes. She had her own little shop in the middle of the High Street and its shining bow windows were always full of cottage loaves, apricot tarts and mince pies, as well as the famous cherry cakes and gingerbread men.

Farmer's wives came in their pony traps to buy her goods, and little schoolboys saved up their pennies to try her pastries.

Betsy had always been so busy, either up to her elbows in flour in the bakehouse, or serving behind the shop counter, that she had never found time to marry; her chief companion in life was Perkin. Perkin was a huge black cat with great green eyes and a grin like the Cheshire Cat — and he had cause to smile!

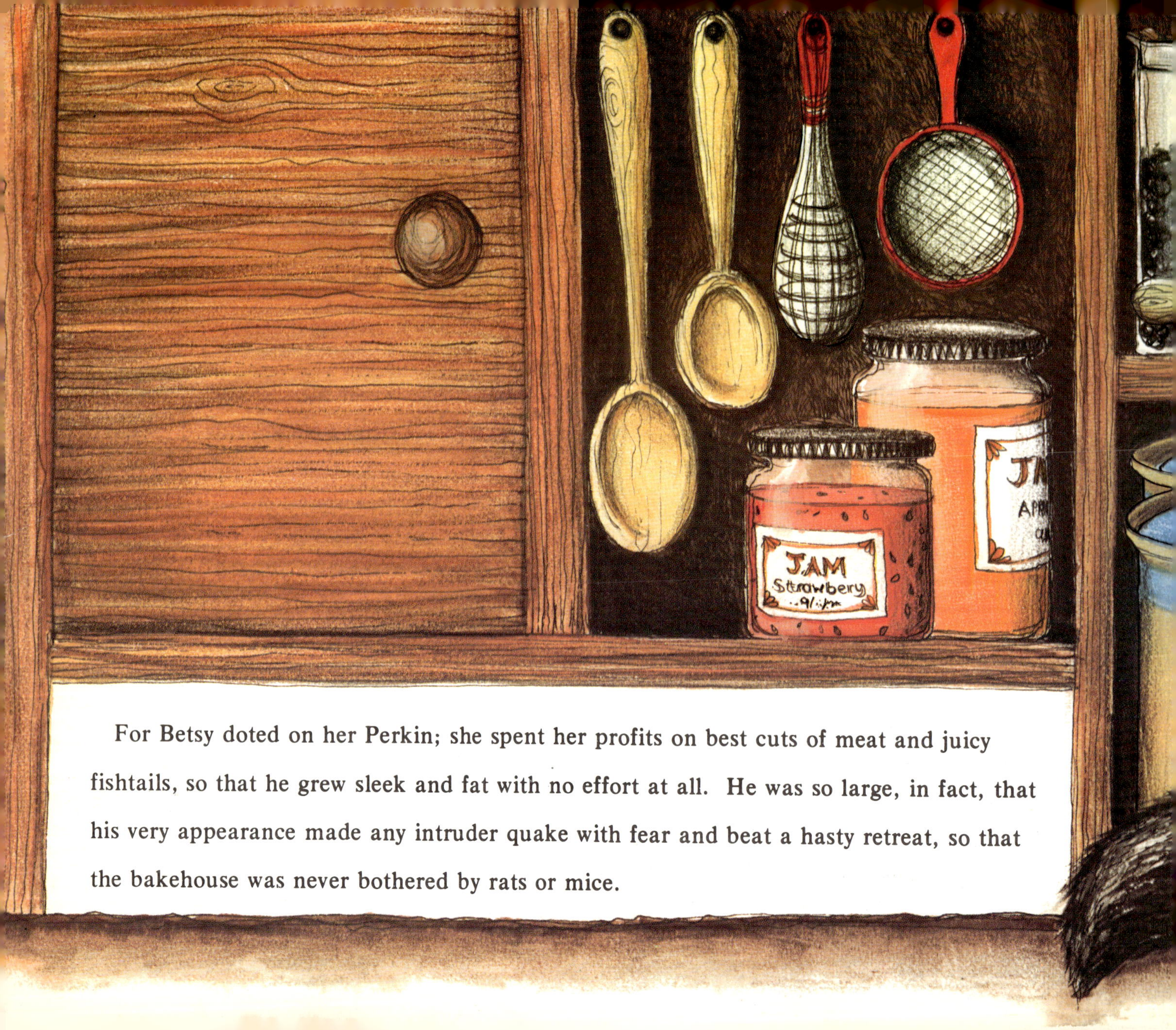

For Betsy doted on her Perkin; she spent her profits on best cuts of meat and juicy fishtails, so that he grew sleek and fat with no effort at all. He was so large, in fact, that his very appearance made any intruder quake with fear and beat a hasty retreat, so that the bakehouse was never bothered by rats or mice.

Now it happened one day that Cressida, a witch from some miles away, had cause to visit Much Twittering, and as she hobbled down the High Street she paused in front of Betsy's shop and admired all the good things in the window. She decided to sample some, and was amazed to find the shop overflowing with customers; the little brass bell never stopped jangling on its spring over the door.

RES 4873
BETSY
BUN

Back home Cressida ate the bread and cake, leaving not a crumb.

"Why, if only I could bake like that, I could live in luxury all my days," she mused. "It's a pity my spell book can't help me." She sat pondering for a long time, then at last she snapped her fingers. She had heard the customers teasing Betsy about Perkin's laziness — and that gave her a wonderful idea.

"I'll turn myself into a little mouse and hide under the bakery table. There I can learn all Betsy's secrets. Then I can come back and set up my own shop." Rubbing her hands gleefully she hurried to her workshop to consult her magic books.

The very next day she changed herself into a mouse and as the last customer left Betsy's shop she scampered in under the counter and through to the bakehouse beyond, where she settled down under a table. When Perkin strolled in she nearly jumped out of her skin, but he didn't even notice her as, stretched on a velvet cushion, he washed his black face.

When the shop closed, Betsy hurried in to do her cooking for the following day. She got out her blue and white mixing bowl, her rolling pin and pastry board, great bins of flour, sugar and fruit, pots of jam and packets of yeast, lard and butter, and last of all her weighing scales. Cressida took note of all these.

BUTTER
BUTTER

"It's the bread rolls first tonight, Perkin," she said. "Now, what do I need? 10 lbs. of flour, yeast . . ." murmured Betsy as she popped everything into the bowl. She was so busy she didn't hear Cressida squeakily echoing everything under the table.

"Well, that's that," she exclaimed at last, wiping her flour-covered fingers on her apron. "While the dough's rising I'll make the apricot tarts. That's 5 lbs. of flour, 2½ lbs. of lard . . ." Again, had she paused, she might have heard tiny squeaks from under the table but Betsy was far too busy to notice.

It was very late when at last she blew out the candles in the bakehouse and opened the shop door to let Perkin take his nightly stroll and she was too tired to notice a little mouse scamper out after him.

For the next few days Cressida was very busy indeed . . .

"Kindly deliver one sack of flour, twenty-four packets of dried fruit, twenty large jars of apricot jam, fifteen pounds of lard, and . . . oh, yes, ten packets of yeast," she told the grocer. He was so amazed his pencil nearly jumped out from behind his ear, but before he could speak Cressida announced that she was opening a bakery.

"But I didn't know you could cook, Cressie," he said.

"Then come and try some of my wares tomorrow," she replied.

The next day a hand-painted sign over her front door announced "Cressida Cook, Confectioner and Baker of Fine Breads."

"We didn't know you could cook, Cressie," exclaimed everyone.

"Then come in and sample my wares," she replied sweetly, opening her front door.

Everyone flocked in, and after tasting her pastries had to agree that Cressida was indeed a very good cook.

"Why, she's as good as Betsy Bun," declared one in surprise.

"And she's nearer," remarked another.

"No need to get the pony and trap out now," smiled another.

Very soon poor Betsy began to worry about her lack of customers, and then someone told her about Cressida's shop.

"But she couldn't cook for toffee," sniffed Betsy disgustedly.

"Oh, but she can," said old Mrs. Jones, "as well as you can, Betsy dear . . . very much like you, in fact. And of course she's a lot nearer some folk than you are." Betsy was not the only one to suffer, for Perkin began to look quite skinny as the money for his meat rations dwindled.

"Well, Perkin," declared Betsy one day. "Cressie is up to no good. Cooks like me are born and not made. I must do something to win my customers back: I'll try making a new cake and see what happens."

At this news Perkin looked a little more cheerful. For days Betsy worked on her new cake mixture, until it was quite perfect. On baking day she put a large sign in her shop window inviting old and new customers to try a free slice of her new cake. Everyone had to agree that it was simply delicious and many declared that Cressida could not possibly make one so good.

Betsy was delighted, but Cressida was furious. There was only one thing for her to do. That evening, there she was in Betsy's bakehouse, a mouse once more.

But she had forgotten one thing — and that was Perkin. He was no longer fat, but skinny and hungry and eager to leap on the tiniest morsel. Suddenly he spotted Cressida busily repeating Betsy's recipe under that table and she was concentrating so hard that she didn't notice the cat creeping up on her.

"Help, help," she squealed as Perkin pounced, and Betsy stopped her mixing just in time to hear her. "Well, I never," she exclaimed. "A talking mouse." She took a closer look. "Why, I do declare, it's the image of Cressida." Betsy grinned. Now she knew why Cressida was such a good cook!

"What shall we do with her, Perkin," she said.

"Oh please," begged the mouse. "It's me, Cressida. I know I've been very wicked, but please, please don't let Perkin eat me. I'll do anything you wish."

"Drop her, Perkin dear," commanded Betsy. "You've no need to catch your own food any more, has he Cressie?"

"No, no," quavered the witch, "I'll close my shop and leave you in peace."

Perkin let her go and she rushed out of the door like a streak of lightning.

Betsy bent down and stroked her cat proudly. "Well, Perkin," she told him. "In a few minutes you've earned your keep for all your nine lives. As for Cressie, I think she has learned her lesson."

And she was right. As soon as she changed back into human form Cressie took down her shop sign and sent all her customers to Betsy. So once more did old Perkin grow fat and sleek and never again did he have to pounce on spying mice!